CRAYOLA HOLI COLORS

WITHDRAWN

ROBIN NELSON

LERNER PUBLICATIONS ◆ MINNEAPOLIS

Content consultant: Radha Balasubramanian, Professor of Russian and Director of Global Studies, University of Nebraska-Lincoln

Official Licensed Product
Lerner Publications Company
A division of Lerner Publishing Group, Inc.
241 First Avenue North
Minneapolis, MN 55401 USA

For reading levels and more information, look up this title at www.lernerbooks.com.

Main body text set in Billy Infant Regular 24/30.
Typeface provided by SparkyType.

Library of Congress Cataloging-in-Publication Data

Names: Nelson, Robin, 1971- author.
Title: Crayola ® Holi colors / Robin Nelson.
Description: Minneapolis : Lerner Publications, 2018. | Series: Crayola ® holiday colors | Includes bibliographical references and index.
Identifiers: LCCN 2018006631 (print) | LCCN 2017046668 (ebook) | ISBN 9781541512474 (eb pdf) | ISBN 9781541510944 (lb : alk. paper) | ISBN 9781541527508 (pb : alk. paper)
Subjects: LCSH: Holi (Hindu festival)—Juvenile literature. | Hinduism—Customs and practices—Juvenile literature.
Classification: LCC BL1239.82.H65 (print) | LCC BL1239.82.H65 N45 2018 (ebook) | DDC 294.5/36—dc23

LC record available at https://lccn.loc.gov/2018006631

Manufactured in the United States of America
1-43978-33992-1/10/2018

TABLE OF CONTENTS

Holi Is Here   4

Colors of Holi   8

Colors in Nature   16

Food and Festival   20

Copy and Color!   28
Glossary   30
To Learn More   31
Index   32

HOLI IS HERE

Holi is a festival of colors.

People celebrate this holiday in spring.

People celebrate Holi in India, Nepal, and many other countries.

Holi is a day for love and friendship.

It is a day to have fun!

COLORS OF HOLI

PURPLE, **YELLOW**, **GREEN**, and **RED**.

People buy colored powders to celebrate Holi.

People surprise friends and strangers.

They throw colored powder into the air and at one another.

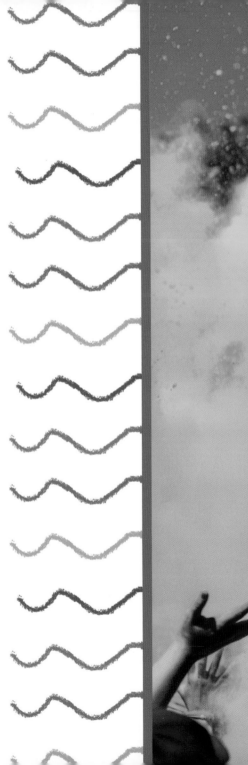

What colors do you see?

Some people throw colored water too.

They use water balloons and sprayers.

Watch out!
You might get wet!

GREEN, **BLUE**, and **PURPLE** cover people's hands and faces.

Colors fill the air. **RED** is all around.

COLORS IN NATURE

Holi celebrates the colors of nature.

People once made colored powders from plants and flowers.

RED and ORANGE flowers made bright red and orange dyes.

This spice is called turmeric.

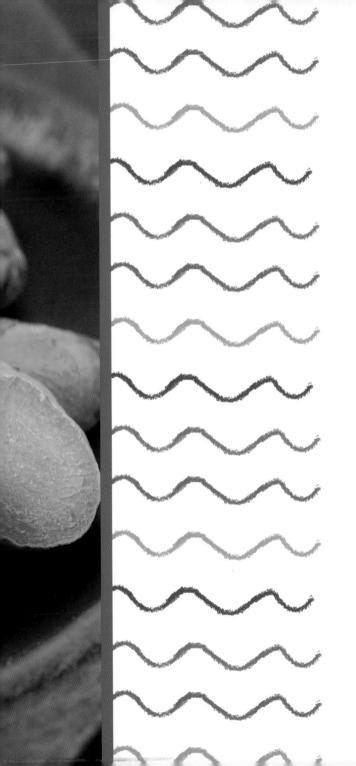

A spice made **YELLOW** dye.

The spice comes from a plant.

FOOD AND FESTIVAL

During Holi, celebration fills the streets!

People sell sweet treats.

This woman makes strings of sugary candy.

Family and friends share fried snacks.
They are **GOLDEN BROWN** and crispy.

Some popular Holi snacks are called *kachori*.

Do you feel like dancing?

Boom, boom!

Someone bangs a **PURPLE** drum.

People start to dance.

Holi is fun and colorful!

Which colors do you like best?

COPY AND COLOR!

Here are some Crayola® crayon colors used in this book. Can you find all of these colors in the photos? Copy these pages, and color the symbols of Holi.

COTTON CANDY

VIVID TANGERINE

SCREAMIN' GREEN

VIVID VIOLET

TURQUOISE

GLOSSARY

celebrate: to do something special or enjoyable for a holiday or important event. A celebration is something like a party that is organized for a holiday or important event.

crispy: dry and crunchy

dyes: substances used to change the color of something

festival: a celebration

fried: cooked in hot oil

nature: everything in the world that isn't made by people. Plants, animals, and the weather are parts of nature.

spice: something used in cooking to add flavor

TO LEARN MORE

BOOKS

Moon, Walt K. *Let's Explore India.* Minneapolis: Lerner Publications, 2017.
Learn about one country where Holi is celebrated.

Pettiford, Rebecca. *Holi.* Minneapolis: Jump!, 2017.
Read about Holi and how people celebrate this festival.

Sharma, Nick. *Holi, the Festival of Colors.* Gleneden Beach, OR: Penman Productions, 2016.
Join Shalu and Preeya as they learn the meaning of friendship while celebrating Holi.

WEBSITES

Holi
https://www.activityvillage.co.uk/holi
Find coloring pages and activities to help you celebrate and learn more about Holi.

Holi, Festival of Colors
http://www.crayola.com/crafts/holi-festival-of-colors-craft/
Have fun with colors and create your own bright Holi pictures.

National Geographic Kids: Holi Festival
http://kids.nationalgeographic.com/explore/holi/#holi-hands.jpg
Explore photographs of the Holi festival.

INDEX

dancing, 25
drum, 25
dye, 17, 19

nature, 16

powder, 9–10, 17

snack, 22
spring, 4

PHOTO ACKNOWLEDGMENTS

The images in this book are used with the permission of: © Gurpreet singh Ranchi/flickr.com (CC BY-SA 3.0), p. 1; Kate Moskvina/ Shutterstock.com, pp. 2, 30, 31, 32 (splash drops pattern); triloks/E+/Getty Images, p. 4; Poras Chaudhary/Stone/Getty Images, p. 5 (top left); Rudra Narayan Mitra/Shutterstock.com, p. 5 (top right); Sean Caffreyr/Lonely Planet Images/Getty Images, p. 5 (bottom left); alexreynolds/Shutterstock.com, p. 5 (bottom right); mmntz/flickr.com (CC 1.0 PDM), pp. 6–7; dutourdumonde/iStock/ Getty Images, p. 9; Mikhail Klyoshev/Shutterstock.com, pp. 10–11; Intellistudies/Shutterstock.com, p. 12; t-lorien/E+/Getty Images, p. 14; Harjeet Singh Narang/Shutterstock.com, p. 15; prwstd/iStock/Getty Images, p. 16; © Wie146/flickr.com (CC BY-SA 3.0), p. 17; NADKI/Shutterstock.com, pp. 18–19; NOAH SEELAM/AFP/Getty Images, p. 21; espies/Shutterstock.com, p. 22; DipaliS/iStock/Getty Images, p. 23; ferrantraite/E+/Getty Images, p. 24; THEPALMER/iStock/Getty Images, p. 25; hadynyah/E+/Getty Images, p. 26; triloks/iStock/Getty Images, p. 27; Laura Westlund/Independent Picture Service, pp. 28, 29 (illustrations).

Cover: Narender9/Wikimedia Commons (CC BY-SA 3.0) (temple); Aparna Balasubramanian/Wikimedia Commons (CC BY-SA 4.0) (beverage); Sun_Shine/Shutterstock.com (powder); kronnui/Shutterstock.com (flowers).